You can *Destroy* the C

You can *Destroy* the Gates of Hell

by Dr. Lester Sumrall

YOU CAN DESTROY THE GATES OF HELL
ISBN 0-937580-68-6

Sumrall Publishing Company, Inc.
P.O. Box 12
South Bend, Indiana 46624

DEDICATION

This book is dedicated to my elder brother,
Rev. W.H. Sumrall
who assisted me so greatly in the doctrinal
truths of the Bible,
when my life was young and tender.

CONTENTS

INTRODUCTION

ARE YOU READY?
LET'S GO!

This book is written because there are millions of people who do not realize the actual presence, personality and power of the devil. Others are like the proverbial ostrich. They wish to hide their heads in the sand as they deny the existence of Satan altogether, even though they know better. Or, they protest that he should be neither discussed nor disturbed.

If we believe the Bible to be true, and that *All scripture is given by inspiration of God, and is profitable for doctrine, for reproof, for correction, for instruction in righteousness.* (II Tim. 3:16), then we must admit that there is much in it that points to the devil as a personal entity. Not only every writer of the New Testament, but, Jesus Himself, tells us about the evil one. It is, therefore, imperative that we understand who he is and what he is up to.

The devil rules the kingdom of darkness, organizes and commands hordes of demons and fallen angels, possesses realms of power, and maintains strongholds by deceiving nations, cities, groups, and individuals. The gates of his kingdom seek to withstand and overcome the Church of the Living God.

When Jesus declared concerning His Church that . . .*the gates of hell shall not prevail against it* (Matt. 16:18b), He was proclaiming that every formidable fortress of Satan falls flat before the legions of the redeemed marching victoriously under the banner of His cross.

May you be greatly inspired by this book, *You Can Destroy the Gates of Hell,* to move into the battlefield of victory in the Lord Jesus Christ, having divine assurance that, *If God be for us, who can be against us!* (Romans 8:31).

Our Leader and Commander-in-Chief, the Lord Jesus Christ, has not conscripted a passive Church-Army. He rejects a status quo church. He cannot use a church that is holding the fort behind closed doors.

Christ said, *Go ye into all the world. . .*
Heal the sick, cleanse the lepers,
raise the dead, cast out devils. . .
Lo, I am with you always, even unto
the end. . . (Mark 16:15; Matt. 10:8; 28:20).

Are you ready? Let's go!

PART ONE

When Jesus came into the coasts of Cæsarea Philippi, he asked his disciples, saying, Whom do men say that I the Son of man am?

And they said, Some say that thou art John the Baptist: some, Elias; and others, Jeremias, or one of the prophets.

He saith unto them, But whom say ye that I am?

And Simon Peter answered and said, Thou art the Christ, the Son of the living God.

And Jesus answered and said unto him, Blessed art thou, Simon Bar-jona: for flesh and blood hath not revealed it unto thee, but my Father which is in heaven.

And I say also unto thee, That thou art Peter, and upon this rock I will build my church; and the gates of hell shall not prevail against it.

And I will give unto thee the keys of the kingdom of heaven: and whatsoever thou shalt bind on earth shall be bound in heaven: and whatsoever thou shalt loose on earth shall be loosed in heaven.

Then charged he his disciples that they should tell no man that he was Jesus the Christ (Matt. 16:13-20).

The Son Of Man

Jesus, walking down a dusty road with His evangelistic team of twelve apostles, arrived at the city of Cæsarea-Philippi at the mouth of the Jordan River. He paused for a moment and said: *Whom do men say that I the Son of man am?* (Matt. 16:13).

I like the designation by which our Lord identified Himself—the Son of man. The Son of God became the Son of man to make us the sons of God! Seventy-nine times throughout the Gospels, Jesus declared Himself to be the Son of man, thereby identifying with the problems of mankind.

As the Son of man, He healed the sick, He fed the hungry, He wept with the bereaved. He understands our weaknesses and our frailties, in *all points tempted like as we are* (Heb. 4:15). He is the true Son of man. He is the acme of manhood. He is the apex of manliness–the highest, the tallest, the noblest of men. He is the perfect example of what God ordained man to be.

Jesus knew Himself to be the Son of God, but humbly identified Himself as the Son of man in order to lead and guide humanity by His example. He also realized that the Jews did not know that He was the fulfillment of prophecy–the promised Messiah of Israel. He did not ask what the Scribes and Pharisees were saying about Him. He wanted to know what the common people thought about the miracles that followed Him wherever He went. Therefore, He said: *Whom do men say that I the Son of man am?* (vs. 13).

And they said, Some say that thou art John the Baptist: some, Elias; and others Jeremias, or one of the prophets. (vs. 14).

Everywhere they went, the disciples heard the subject discussed, and had often questioned among themselves, "Who is He?"

Some believed Him to be the ghost of John the Baptist, who had been beheaded by Herod Antipas for preaching repentance.

Others thought the prophecy in Malachi 4:5, that God would send the Prophet Elijah back to them, was fulfilled in this man.

Because of His preaching, still others believed Him to be Jeremiah resurrected, or one of the other prophets, perhaps Moses.

Unless the apostles were hedging, it is interesting that their answers seemed to infer that everybody thought Jesus was not an ordinary man, but someone who had been raised from the dead.

The answers did not satisfy Jesus. They meant that the people were confused about His person and, therefore, had no true comprehension of what He had come to do for them. We know who You are!

Even more important than the opinions of the general populace were the responses of His own followers.

He saith unto them, But whom say ye that I am? And Simon Peter answered and said, Thou art the Christ, the Son of the living God (vs. 15-16).

No doubt, John the beloved was ready to answer. Philip possibly would have said something if he had been fast enough. Andrew would have been glad to make a statement, but Peter instantly broke the silence. By temperament, he seemed to be the spokesman for the group, and the answer flowed from Peter like a gushing river. Since the time Jesus had come to them walking on the water (Matt. 14:25-33), they were sure that He was a Son of God, but now the words came from Peter like an explosion.

We know who you are! You are the Christ, the Messiah, the Son of the living God! You are the One who is promised to Israel!

Peter's confession is the greatest single declaration ever made by man throughout history. It forever identified Jesus of Nazareth as the Christ of God. Around that one statement have been fought the greatest word-battles in all the ages of Christendom.

The mystery was revealed. Jesus of Nazareth was none other than the exclusive, unique, only-begotten of the Father in heaven. He was born by the mysterious fatherhood of God which no human intellect has fully comprehended—born before the universe was created in the infinite past, so remote that no chronicle of events concerning it has been released. But somewhere in the throne room of eternity, Elohim conceived a son and cried, Thou art the Christ, the Son of the living God! And in this instant of time God revealed that truth to Peter and the others. Yes, Jesus, Thou art the Christ, the Son of the living God!

The Turning Point

This is the turning point of the Synoptic Gospels. From this moment on, Jesus begins to fulfill the prophecies of His death.

And Jesus answered and said unto him, Blessed art thou, Simon Bar-jona: for flesh and blood hath not revealed it unto thee, but my Father which is in heaven (vs. 17).

Peter had not come to this decision by study or by instruction, not by nature or by education, neither by wit nor by human wisdom. Flesh and blood had not revealed it to him. God the Father in heaven revealed it to him by His Spirit. It was revelation knowledge, and Peter, therefore, was blessed because of it.

The Apostle Paul also confessed that he *conferred not with flesh and blood* (Gal. 1:16), but received revelation knowledge of the gospel directly from God.

There are things we learn from heaven that we can never learn here on earth. There are truths from heaven that are not taught in school. If we were to learn them, we must receive them straight from God.

When we speak by divine revelation, we are all blessed. Any time we can tell what

God is thinking, what God is doing, what God is going to do, we are blessed by bringing forth revelation knowledge from God to the people.

No one truly knows Christ except by divine revelation. We do not get to know Him through a sermon or by studying a book. True, we can get to know about Him that way, but we come to know Him in a personal way only when the Holy Spirit reveals Him to us as the unique Son of God.

Divine Revelation

I was born and raised in a full-gospel church. During my youth I heard every kind of sermon imaginable about salvation and the atonement. But years later, when I was ministering in Brazil, I stood up one night to preach about the cross. Suddenly, in a vision, I saw Calvary and I was overwhelmed by the glory of it.

I stood before the congregation and wept, as I tried to describe to the people what I was seeing, and the congregation wept in the presence of God's power for an hour and a half as I presented to them, under the anointing of the Holy Spirit, an exposition of God's love at Calvary.

Mentally, I already knew much about Calvary, but when it came to a divine revelation of the awesomeness of Calvary and the majesty of the Son of God suspended between the heavens and the earth, I received it in my spirit by revelation.

God is not dead. People who say He is are the ones who are dead—spiritually dead, *dead in trespasses and sins* (Eph. 2:1). Their spirits have not been quickened. Their souls have not been revived. They have not received revelation knowledge of Calvary.

Peter was spiritually alive. He did not get his information at the feet of Rabbi Gamaliel in Jerusalem. He did not learn it at the School of Theology in Galilee. He heard directly from the throne room of God in heaven.

A New Creature In Christ

When I was in Japan, a man asked me to tell him what had happened to his housemaid. He had hired an uneducated, inexperienced Japanese girl from a rural area to clean his home, but she seemed unable to learn to do anything well. The girl was invited to a Christian mission where she received Jesus Christ as her Lord and Savior, and within a few weeks was instructing her employer in the way he should live.

The man said to me, "I'm not only a university graduate, but I have studied the great historical books of culture about my people, and here this ignorant and unlearned maid rebukes me and tells me how to live. Now she does everything well. A few months ago she could not even make a bed. What happened to her?"

"She was born again," I said, "She is not the same person she used to be. A new person now lives in your house, and God has shown her these things."

Peter, A Rock Among Lively Stones

And I say also unto thee, That thou art Peter, and upon this rock I will build my church; and the gates of hell shall not prevail against it (vs. 18).

Two Greek words are used here: *Petros,* meaning rock, and *petra,* meaning boulder.

Jesus said to Peter, *This know, that you are a little stone, but upon this boulder of your confession I will build My church.* Build His Church upon what? Upon the revelation given to Peter, upon the proposition that He is *the Christ, the Son of the living God.*

In I Peter 2:5-6, we read where Peter himself writes:

Ye [Christians] *also, as lively stones, are built up a spiritual house, an holy priesthood. . .Wherefore also. . .I lay in Sion a chief corner stone* [Jesus]. . .

As Peter was one stone, so we are also stones in the Church, with Jesus Christ as the *head of the corner* (vs. 7), the chief cornerstone.

Jesus also said that He, not another, would build His Church. The Church of the Lord Jesus Christ cannot be built by or upon any human being. It is built upon the eternal proposition that our Father God in heaven gave His only Son, and that the Son gave His life on Calvary to save the world from sin. That truth is the nucleus of the Church.

Power To The Church

After His crucifixion and resurrection, Jesus

Christ sent to the Church the power of the Holy Spirit, that the "gates of hell" (or the "powers of death") should not prevail against it. It was through His death that He was able to *deliver them* [the Church] *who through fear of death were all their lifetime subject to bondage* (Heb. 2:15), and send to them *the promise of the Father* (Acts 1:4), the power of the Holy Spirit (vs. 8)—not to Peter's Church, but to the Church of Jesus Christ.

PART TWO

The Gates To The City

Why does Jesus speak of gates? Because it is through the gates that people and power interact with one another. It is through the gates of the city that the army pours forth to attack the enemy, and it is back through the gates of the city that the conquering army comes to take a prey.

Ancient cities invariably had gates and walls to protect the citizens from intruders—robbers, murders and enemy invaders. Through the centuries, the strongest defense of many a great city has been the strength of its gates. The stronger the gates, the more secure the state. City gates were made to withstand fire, battering rams, swords and spears, arrows and catapulted rocks, and were often covered with metal and garishly painted and engraved with grotesque heathen deities, supposedly guarding the city. Huge gates for horsemen and chariots often framed smaller gates for people on foot.

I have lived in parts of the world where the gates meant the difference between life and death. When I went to Tibet on muleback, every town we slept in had practically impenetrable gates. I got locked out once or twice by arriving after dark, and had to bang and beat and scream and yell before the keeper would let me in, because when the sun goes down, the gates are locked for the night.

Gates are often synonymous with prestige, riches and power. In Peking, China, the imposing red gates to the Forbidden City surrounding the Emperor's palace strike awe in the beholder.

Political Gates

Behind the gates of a city, politics and policies are formed.

In Bible times the city gates were often used as the place for government transactions and the seat of civil power. In Genesis 19:1, we find Abraham's nephew Lot sitting as one of the aldermen in the gates of Sodom, occupying a position of judicial power. In the Book of Ruth, when Boaz wanted Ruth for his wife, he went to the aldermen and rulers of the city who were seated in conference at the gates.

Gates were then and still are used as places to transact business. Today, at the Damascus Gate, the northern entrance to the Old City of Jerusalem, there is always the chance for a big business deal. The walls are only a few yards wide, but ten or more merchants do business within the gates. They arrive early, as soon as the gates are opened, and they stay late, knowing that the tourists will see them first on the way in and hear them last on the way out. To the businessman, the gate is a prized location.

Military Gates

The ramparts of the ancient world were citadels of military maneuvering. The strategists, surrounded by their mighty warriors, met in the gates to debate the latest schemes for conquering cities and enemy kingdoms. Nations rose and fell according to the wisdom or foolishness of the decisions made in the gates.

The Gates Of Heaven

According to the Bible, there are gates to heaven and gates to hell.

The Book of Revelation states that there are twelve gates to the New Jerusalem, each gate made from one pearl. God did not show John, the writer of the book, gates of diamonds because diamonds come into being by a process of pressure upon carbon deep within the earth. Pearls result from pain, intense suffering, when a grain of sand enters the shell of an oyster, and the oyster suffers grating and grinding pain in its body.

The entrance to heaven through the gates of pearl is not free, but Christ has paid the price. He paid for the pearl-gates to heaven by the intense grinding pain and suffering He endured on the cross. Therefore, the redeemed of the Lord will joyfully dance through the gates of glittering pearl, but when they meet Jesus, they will see the nail prints in His feet and in the palms of His hands, the scar in His side, and the marks of thorns across His brow; the unhealing marks of the sacrifice of Christ for our salvation and entrance into heaven.

The Gates Of Hell

Behind the gates of hell, the fortress that locks in the dead and locks out the would-be deliverers, the powers and policies of darkness and death are conceived; to oppose the gospel, to corrupt the people, to persecute God's ministers, and to root out the name of Christianity by subtlety and by force. These gory gates are battlescarred by countless frantic victims striving to escape.

The Church of Christ is not on the defensive; it is an offensive army. Christ said of His Church that the gates of hell could not prevail against it. His Church is a strong, militant, courageous army against which no power of evil can stand.

The gates of hell, like the gates of heaven, are not only to be understood as physical, geographical gates, but also as gates of the soul and gates of the spirit.

Hell's Geographical Gates

There are actual geographical locations where the devil sits and rules as supreme king and judge. Christ said to the church at Pergamos, in Revelation 2:13:

I know thy works and where thou dwellest, even where Satan's seat is: and thou holdest fast my name, and hast not denied my faith, even in those days wherein Antipas was my faithful martyr, who was slain among you, where Satan dwelleth.

Antipas was a real man, who was actually slain in the city of Pergamos for his witness to Christ.

I have discovered by experience that there are cities closed to the gospel of deliverance. Where the magistrates are resistant and the people listless towards the gospel message, tremendous revival crusade efforts hardly make a ripple.

In Calcutta, for instance, a city named for the powerful and evil goddess Kali, demon power is strongly and deeply entrenched. It is not difficult to feel darkness and oppression upon entering that city of approximately nine million people, where some churches have worked for years, and are still struggling for existence.

The Church must face these geographical areas with faith and the supernatural power of the Holy Spirit in order to destroy the devil's hold upon them.

Paul says in Ephesians 6:12, *For we*

wrestle not against flesh and blood, but against principalities, against powers, against the rulers of the darkness of this world, against spiritual wickedness in high places. Our battle is not with the people, but with the evil one. Jesus said in Matthew 12:29, that we must *first bind the strong man, and then. . .spoil his house.* Otherwise, our missionary work will be disappointing and ineffective.

For many years the desire of my heart has been to see aggressive full-gospel evangelistic centers in all the big cities of the world, from which to preach deliverance with apostolic fervor, to tear down the gates of the devil, and to lift high the standard of the redeeming gospel of Jesus Christ.

Hell's Soulish Gates of Immorality

Multitudes today are slaves to immorality, the sensual sins of the flesh. Impulses which they cannot control bind them. The devil imprisons them with filthy and evil habits from which they are unable to extricate themselves by their own strength or willpower. They are the hellish gates of the "new morality," which is nothing more than the old immorality.

It is ridiculous to accost an alcoholic with the statement, "Stop drinking and live for Jesus." He cannot do it. The tormenting spirit of alcoholism must first be bound and cast out before he can even make the decision whether or not he wants to be free.

If he does not want to stay free, the demon is glad to have him back!

Mary Magdalene stayed free. Jesus cast seven demons out of her and she stayed free because she had a heart for God. It was to her, the prisoner set free, that Jesus first showed Himself after His resurrection (Mark 16:9).

Hell's Soulish Gate Of Gambling

Gambling is one of the gates of hell which holds multitudes of prisoners behind its evil, forbidding barricades. That lecherous spirit fastens itself upon the mind, the soul and the spirit of its prisoner, making him forsake family, love, decency, honesty and Christ to satisfy his lust and serve Satan at the seat of mere chance.

Hell's Spiritual Gate Of Apostasy

Apostasy is among the spiritual gates of hell.

Now the Spirit speaketh expressly, that in the latter times some shall depart from the faith, giving heed to seducing spirits, and doctrines of devils (1 Tim. 4:1).

Apostasy is the perversion of truth in the form of religion. To make apostasy convincing, the devil takes truth and gives it a twist. It is God's Word that is true, not some man or some devil's interpretation. God's supernatural power must break down the devil's gate of apostasy before the deceived can believe they have been deceived, and receive the true light.

Hell's Gate Of Spiritism

Spiritism is one of the gates of apostasy. Its dark, closeted lies about conversing with dead friends and beloved family members become chains of darkness. Spiritism is not revealed and defeated by argument or traditional church services but by the miraculous power delivered to God's victorious Church.

Cults, The Gates Of Hell

Multitudes today are being enticed into the new demonic cults of our day. They attract the spiritually ignorant and the spiritually dead, professing Christians. Once they are enslaved and shackled by worshiping demons or men, only the power of deliverance by the Holy Spirit through the Church of the Lord Jesus Christ can smash the barbed gates and set them free. Again, let me say, that the battle is not with the people, but with the spiritual forces of evil, and must be fought by spiritual warfare.

Philosophy, A Gate Of Hell

The philosophy of humanism/atheism is one of the most insiduous gates of hell, because it sounds so good, but it is anti-Christian, anti-truth, and anti-gospel, and therefore unacceptable. Millions are in hell or on the way to hell because of the philosophy of humansim, which is atheistic to the core.

Many churches today, professing themselves to be Christian churches, teach the doctrine of humanism, in which the good deeds of a man are rewards in themselves, and heaven and hell are right here on earth. Denominational doctrines cannot get through to the atheist. Christian philosophers cannot destroy atheism. Only the moving, militant, praying, powerful Church of Jesus Christ can demonstrate God's power to smash the gates of atheistic unbelief and cry, ''Gates fall down! Let there be faith in the heart of the atheist!''

The Nazism of World War II was a branch of the evil philosophy of humanism. Communism is another. Today the face of communism is changing, but there are still people who would die for communism this very moment. These people are actually possessed by the devil. The prayers of God's people have been answered in seeing the spirit of revolutionary Marxism broken in Eastern Europe. Only Christ can set people free from the lies of these atheistic forces. Surely evil philosophers and rulers are from the ramparts of hell itself.

Superstition, A Gate Of Hell

Superstition is another gate of hell, a heavy spiritual burden to which the devil adds daily. "Old wives' tales" concerning black cats crossing one's path, walking under ladders, tossing spilled salt over the left shoulder, all take their toll by putting fear in the heart of the superstitious person. I am not afraid of a dozen black cats crossing my path. I walk under any ladder I feel like walking under. And on Friday the 13th I am just as active as at any other time. Any way the devil can put us under bondage, he will, and superstition is just one more way. He's been amazingly successful in the Orient where streets are deliberately laid out in winding and crooked paths. Why not straight? The people believe that then the devil could follow them home. In Japan, bridges over small streams are built like steep steps up and down. Why? Because that way, the devil, who can only move in a straight line, could not pursue.

Christians are to be free from superstition because we have the promise of Christ, that *If the Son shall make you free, ye shall be free indeed* (John 8:36).

The Tormenting Gate Of Fear

There is a higher percentage of fearful people in the world today than at any other time in history. In non-Christian nations, the heathen are burdened with fears—afraid of the day, afraid of the night, afraid of the field, afraid of the city. The pagan lives in terror. Only God can break the torment of fear and set him free, *For God hath not given us the spirit of fear; but of power, and of love, and of a sound mind* (II Tim. 1:7).

In America today, millions of people are bound by fear, not knowing how to get free. Medicine and doctors are not helping them rid themselves permanently of fear. Daily we receive pitiful letters from fearful people, even strong men with hearts filled with fear. Lives have been destroyed by this example of the gates of hell.

It is not enough to say to a fearful person, "Do not be afraid! Do not act like a child!" Fear is real and they need deliverance.

The Bible says in I John 4:18, *perfect love casteth out fear.* Fear anticipates punishment, so the only kind of love that rids us of that fear is the forgiving love of God. When the love of God in Jesus Christ moves into a heart, the devil's fear must go. His black gate of fear is torn down by that love and he is routed.

Some of us are like the little boy who asked his mother to go into the dark kitchen and get him a glass of water.

"You go," his mother said.

"I'm scared to go," he answered.

"Go ahead and get your water," his mother said tenderly. "Jesus will be in the kitchen with you, and nothing can harm you there."

The poor little boy went trembling and shaking into the kitchen, fumbled with the glass and knocked it over. Then his mother heard him say, "Jesus, I know You are here, but please don't move. You'll scare me to death!"

God does not want us to live like that little boy. His Word says, *The just shall live by faith* (Rom. 1:17b), and faith is the opposite, the antithesis of fear.

The Gate Of Demon Possession

The gates of hell had prevailed over the demoniac of Gadara (Mark 5:15), out of whom Jesus cast three thousand demons, thereby restoring him to his right mind. Orthodoxy had not helped him. Legalism had not helped him. Advice had not helped him. The power of God set him free.

That same powere is available to use today. To speak to another of the crucified, risen, glorified, returning Savior is that the hearer may accept Christ and be born again—that is a demonstration of the awesome power of Christ, power that sets people free (see John 14:12).

Mental Illness, From The Gate OF Hell

In this late hour of world history, literally millions of people need to be delivered from mental stress, strain and breakdown. There are more disturbed minds in the world today than ever before in the history of mankind. I have heard it said that in America 18 million people need psychiatric help but are not getting it. That is more people than the combined population of Australia and New Zealand. That is a whole nation of mentally ill people. The minds of these sick people, burdened with trouble and sorrow, need a miracle from God.

Physical Illness, From The Gate Of Hell

Many of our physical ailments are direct results of the problems and sorrows of the world and come straight from the gates of hell. Jesus spent His earthly ministry healing the sick by delivering them from the bondages of the devil that had ruined their health.

The epileptic boy, with the deaf and dumb spirit that had come into him when he was a child, was brought to Jesus, who healed him by rebuking the demon, then lifting the youth up by his hand (Mark 9:17-27).

Jesus healed the hunchback woman with His Word, as seen in Luke 13:11-13.

He healed the woman who had an issue of blood, probably from cancer, when she came to Him with faith (Mark 5:25-34).

Jesus sent power to the Church that we might break the power of the hideous satanic gates to pieces and bring liberty, freedom, peace and joy to humanity, the righteousness of Christ, the peace of God that passes all understanding, and the joy of the Holy Spirit.

PART THREE

The Keys

And I will give unto thee the keys of the kingdom of heaven (Matt. 16:19).

What a remarkable statement! Jesus will deliver to Peter the keys to His Kingdom—*will,* not "does now" or "already has." Jesus gave them something to look forward to, and it happened on the day of Pentecost!

What are the keys for? They are to open doors. No doors, no need for keys. Jesus said to Peter that, because of his divine revelation from the Father of who Jesus really is, and because of Peter's sound confession, that Peter would be the one to lead the way—open the kingdom doors. Not that Peter was to have preeminence over the others, for Peter himself tells us that the elders were to *feed the flock of God. . .neither as being lords over God's heritage, but being examples to the flock* (I Peter 5:2-3). He had heard Jesus say:

Ye know that they which are accounted to rule over the Gentiles exercise lordship over them; and their great ones exercise authority upon them. But so shall it not be among you: but whosoever will be great among you, shall be your minister [servant] (Mark 10:42-43).

Fifty days after Jesus' resurrection, on the day of Pentecost, it was not John's time to preach; it was not James' turn to launch the ministry of the Holy Spirit. It was Peter's time. Jesus had given the keys to Peter, and on that day Peter used the key to open up the gospel to the Jews. And three thousand men walked through that door into the kingdom after a five-minute sermon (Acts 2:14-41). That was a pretty big key!

In Acts, chapter 3, we read of a man who had been lame from birth who was healed (vs. 12-26). In this instance, Peter used the key to perform the first miracle of healing, followed by another teaching-sermon, after which he again preached to the multitudes.

Peter was not made superior to his brethren, but was that one chosen to lead the way in the newly born apostolic Church.

The Keys Of Authority

And whatsoever thou shalt bind on earth

shall be bound in heaven; and whatsoever thou shalt loose on earth shall be loosed in heaven (Matt. 16:18).

This delegated spiritual power and authority was not given only to Peter, but to the other apostles; and it is our glorious privilege as believers today, as faithful witnesses, speaking the Word of God.

It was demonstrated magnificently in the early church, as seen in Acts 4:31 where we read of the place where they were assembled together as being shaken, and they were all filled with the Holy Ghost, ''and they spoke the word of God with boldness.'' The result was a multitude who believed. ''And with great strength and ability and power the apostles delivered their testimony to the resurrection of the Lord Jesus, and great grace—loving kindness and favor and goodwill—rested richly upon them all'' (vs. 33 AMP).

God's Aggressive Church

Let us now declare war on the works of darkness! Let the Church go on the offensive, seeking out trouble, bringing deliverance to mankind and the power of the living God to those in need.

The gates of hell are the devil's gates. The strongest of his defenses are at his gates, whether material or spiritual. So the Church is ready to fight its greatest battles there. At best, the gates are defensive warfare. Satan is on the defensive, so it is time that we take the offensive against him.

Between His death and resurrection, our Lord Jesus Christ went into Hades and wrenched from the devil the keys that He has now given to us through Peter. It is time to storm the gates of hell!

The weapons of our warfare are not carnal, but mighty through God to the pulling down of strongholds. . . (II Cor. 10:4).

The Church of Jesus Christ is not a passive church. It is not a *status quo* church. It is not a church that is holding the fort behind closed doors. It is a church seeking a battlefield, armed and ready to rush the enemy and pursue him and his monsters of hell back to the gates of Christ's authority and calling the prisoners to come forth to freedom.

[God] *is able to do exceeding abundantly above all that we ask or think, according to the power that worketh in us* (Eph. 3:20).

Satan realizes the potential strength of the

victorious Church; he is afraid of the Church. He has built his gates strong to keep his captives in bonds, and he is working hard to keep the Church from realizing that he is not strong enough to withstand any aggression from a band of determined Christians.

Jesus has given us the command and the authority to set the captives free, and it is up to us to obey.

The Offensive Weapon Of Our Warfare

The offensive weapon of our warfare is the Word of God, wielded in the power of the Holy Spirit, in obedience to the will of God. We are commanded to:

Heal the sick, cleanse the lepers, raise the dead, cast out devils (Matt. 10:8).

When Jesus gave the keys to Peter, He said that at that time they were not to reveal His true identity to anyone. It was too soon. He first had to die, crash the gates of hell Himself, then ascend to heaven to send the Holy Spirit upon His Church. It is no longer too early. The Holy Spirit has come and imbued His Church with power.

We Are Not Afraid?

The eternal Church of the Lord Jesus Christ with its pristine anointing and power is not afraid of the works of evil.

We are not afraid of communism and its atheistic boastings.

We are not afraid of the new cults, rising in black confusion. We are not blind to the cloud of Eastern religions seeking to blanket the minds of our people and destroy the true worship of Almighty God. The Eastern religions never brought blessing to the benighted adherent in Oriental lands, and they are certainly no competition for true Christian worship. We do not fear them, for *greater is he that is in you* [us] *than he that is in the world* (I John 4:4).

The Church, founded upon the mighty revelation that Jesus Christ is the Son of God, is not afraid of disease. In the hour in which we live, disease runs rampant through the world. In this hour of scientific excellence, disease runs at a higher pace than ever before. When hospitals and clinics and sanitariums are more numerous than ever, only the Church of Jesus Christ knows the perfect healing Savior who heals the sick and afflicted.

We are not afraid of demon power, whether its manifestations should be in the dense jungles of Africa, on the high snow-crested peaks of Tibet, in smoke-filled opium dens or in swank night clubs where heathen modern man dances to the devil's beat. The Church knows no fear of demon power.

The Church Triumphant

Can you hear the marching feet of the Church Triumphant, marching to victory? Behind it lies nothing but the defeated enemy and his cohorts. The power of the living God has laid them low.

Through the resurrection, *God hath made that same Jesus. . .both Lord and Christ* (Acts 2:36). And we are to follow in His footsteps and do the works He did on earth.

The King of Heaven has triumphed over the king of Hades. You can become a part of His victorious army, crashing the gates of hell, destroying the enemies on every hand, liberating the captives, and realizing fully the hour of destiny in which we live.

Turn away from those who proclaim falsely that "God is dead!" Come out from among those who preach doom! Leave the complacent ones who claim that the "Great Commission'' was for yesterday.

Join with the Church who knows that our Lord Jesus is *the same yesterday, and today, and for ever* (Heb. 13:8).

BELIEVE that the sunset of the Christian Church will be more glorious than its sunrise!

BELIEVE that God is now ready to bare His mighty arm of omnipotence and set the multitudes free!

BELIEVE that Christ, whose banner strikes terror in the hearts of His enemies, whose victories are tremendous, whose joy is supernal, is coming for His bride.

This moment is the most glorious hour of the Christian Church. From now until our coming King bursts the starry dome of heaven, when the trump of God sounds, when the dead in Christ arise from the grave, we will go on in victory. We will first march forward, then, at that great day, we will march upward into heaven, crying:

Hosanna unto Him, who hath
all power in heaven and in earth,
and who has delivered supernatural
power unto His Church, that even
THE GATES OF HELL SHALL NOT
PREVAIL AGAINST IT! AMEN!

CONCLUSION

CHALLENGE

The biggest thing that the gates of hell teaches me is that Christianity is not a defensive mechanism. Much of the Body of Christ is always waiting for the devil to hit. We should hit him first. Aggressive warfare is what God wants a church to have. Hit evil when it is little. Smack wickedness hard. Do not wait for it to become a giant. Attack each situation before it becomes one of the devil's gates. If you wait too long, you have to use all the strength of the whole army to knock the thing down.

The church is not meant to sit in a rocking chair and rock away. Yet, many Christians like to do that. If a preacher becomes a little militant in this country, half his congregation might walk off and leave him. They say, "I don't want to go over there. The pastor is always pointing at somebody.'' If you are not fighting the devil and standing up for God, then you are no good on the face of the earth. We are here as soldiers; we are here as warriors, and we are here as winners. We are winners in Jesus' name.

In the old times the strongest part of a city was its gates. The most fortified part of the city was the gates. The gates were the center of learning, the center of commerce, the center of politics. That is the reason why Jesus speaks of the gates. He did not speak of the wall where someone could climb up a tree and jump over. Instead, He spoke of the strongholds of the city—its gates, where the enemy has all of his artillery. Jesus said, ''Even those gates cannot stand up before you. Go and knock them down.'' The biggest thing he has, the worst thing he has, knock them down.

THE GREAT EXCHANGE

The most important day in human history occurred over two-thousand years ago as Jesus hung on a Roman cross.

God was performing the most profound EXCHANGE that the human mind can conceive: our sinful lives for His sinless life, our rightful place in hell for an undeserved dwelling in heaven!

The very Son of God died to take away your sins. He offers you His righteousness for your sins.

If you have not trusted in the EXCHANGE of His life for yours, open your heart to these truths:

- *All have sinned and fall short of the glory of God* (Romans 3:23).
- *The wages of sin is death, but the gift of God is eternal life through Jesus Christ our Lord* (Romans 6:23).
- *God shows His own love for us in this: While we were still sinners, Christ died for us* (Romans 5:8).
- *If you confess with your mouth, "Jesus is Lord," and in your heart believe that God raised Him from the dead, you will be saved. For it is with the heart that you believe and are justified, and it is with your mouth that you confess and are saved* (Romans 10: 9-10).

There is nothing to fear — the tomb is Empty! Jesus *is* the Son of God, and your sin has been cancelled, if only you will believe and trust in Him.

Accept the sacrifice He made for your sake. Then, invite Him into your heart and make Him Lord of your life, and you will be reborn, a new child of God.

As the picture depicts, Jesus paid the penalty for the sins of everyone in the world. Notice that one criminal (like other believers) accepted the benefit Jesus offered to him. Also, observe how the other criminal (like all unrepentant sinners) rejected the offer of salvation. Ponder the wisdom and the foolishness of this scene as it is played out day by day in the world around us. Consider using this drawing to explain to others about history's most important day.

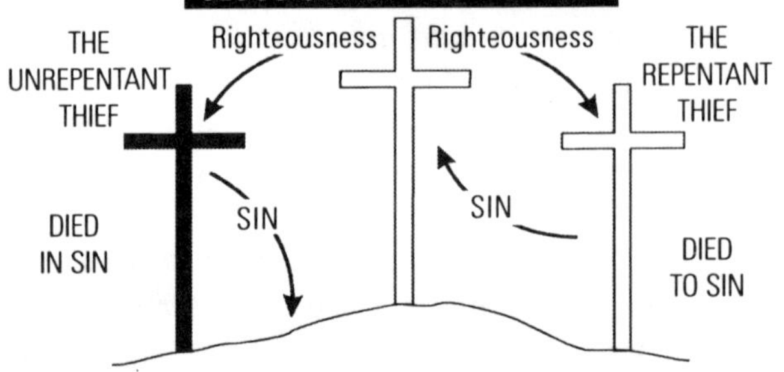

If you have received this gift of life through Jesus, please tell us so we can celebrate with you and send you some materials that will help you walk daily with the Lord. Call us at Prayerline, 24 hours a day, at 219-291-1010.

LeSEA Ministries

In 1957, Lester Sumrall, with the help and support of his family and many friends, founded LeSEA (Lester Sumrall Evangelistic Association). This ministry has subsequently given birth to a multi-faceted outreach.

Christian Center Cathedral of Praise and the LeSEA office complex were dedicated in 1968. The church is the vital support for the extensive ministries that make up LeSEA, Inc. Christian Center remains steadfast in it's commitment to preaching and teaching the Word of God, to ministering to the needs of it's members and the immediate community, and to extending it's influence upon the worldwide Body of Christ. A thriving small-group ministry encourages members to cultivate friendships that confirm and strengthen their faith. In response to God's admonition that we be diligent in teaching the Lord's statutes to our children, Christian Center established Christian Center School (K-12) and Little People's Christian Learning Center, a day-care facility. The church also sponsors a yearly campmeeting and an annual ministers' conference, which attract believers, pastors, and lay ministers from around the world.

LeSEA Broadcasting began with the construction of radio station WHME-FM in South Bend, Indiana in 1967. Under the exceptional leadership of Peter Sumrall, the LeSEA Broadcasting Network has grown to include seven full-power and seven low-power television stations, a national satellite ministry, three FM radio stations, Internet services, and five international shortwave radio stations. The Gospel is broadcast via radio and television twenty-four hours a day, seven days a week, having the potential to reach 100% of the world's population. **LeSEA Tours** conducts semi-annual pilgrimages to the Holy Land, and offers quality service for all destinations. **Prayerline** allows a loving, personal contact with individuals who call for spiritual support and guidance. Trained volunteers staff the 24-hour hotline, and many souls are touched by the healing and redeeming power of God.

LeSEA Global Feed the Hungry® is one of the crowning achievements of Lester Sumrall's ongoing ministry to feed desperately poor families within the Body of Christ. Our mission is to show God's compassion to people in need, to bless "forgotten" members within the Body of Christ, to strengthen the Church, and evangelize the lost. Established in 1987, LeSEA Global Feed the Hungry® annually gives millions of pounds of food and supplies valued at millions of dollars to countless believers around the globe. Following Dr. Sumrall's God-given design, this is a pastor to pastor, church to church program through which supplies are given directly to leaders within the church or church community who in turn give to those experiencing need.

Sumrall Publishing Company publishes, produces, and distributes books, videos, and tapes authored by Dr. Lester Sumrall, Stephen Sumrall, and other Christian leaders. While Lester Sumrall's ministry spanned six decades and reached out to more than 120 countries, his teachings live on in the more than 100 books, tapes, and study guides that remain.

Indiana Christian University is LeSEA's post-secondary education facility. It is accredited by the state of Indiana and grants both undergraduate and graduate degrees for those called to ministry work. ICU also offers a one-year Certificate of Achievement in Charismatic Studies. Video extensions in local churches and correspondence studies for individual students expand the outreach of ICU throughout the world.

Dr. Stephen Sumrall directs the various outreaches of LeSEA, Inc. (LeSEA Global Feed the Hungry, Sumrall Publishing Company, Christian Center School and Day Care, Indiana Christian University) and is Senior Pastor of Christian Center Cathedral of Praise in South Bend, Indiana.

Other books by Dr. Lester Sumrall –

Adventuring With Christ
Angels To Help You
Be Bold and Walk Tall
Courage to Conquer
Demons: The Answer Book
Faith Can Change Your World
The Gifts and Ministries of the Holy Spirit
God's Blueprint for a Happy Home
The Life Story of Lester Sumrall
The Making of a Champion
The Militant Church
Mystery of Death
Pioneers of Faith
Promises Of God
Run With the Vision
Spirit, Soul, and Body
Unprovoked Murder
Victory & Dominion Over Fear
60 Things God Said about Sex
101 Questions & Answers on Demon Power

To receive a catalog of these and other books, audios and videos contact:

Sumrall Publishing
P.O. Box 12, South Bend, IN 46624
www.sumrallpublishing.com